BUCKINGHAMSHIRE
PRIV

by

MARTIN ANDREW

COUNTRYSIDE BOOKS

NEWBURY · BERKSHIRE

First published 1998
© Martin Andrew 1998

All rights reserved. No reproduction
permitted without the prior permission
of the publisher:

COUNTRYSIDE BOOKS
3 Catherine Road
Newbury, Berkshire

ISBN 1 85306 503 X

Produced through MRM Associates Ltd., Reading
Typeset by Techniset Typesetters, Merseyside
Printed by Woolnough Bookbinding Ltd., Irthlingborough

CONTENTS

My very first complete privy, No.22 Great Hampden.

FOREWORD

I must start this book with a confession: I have never used a Buckinghamshire privy in anger. As a Conservation Officer I have seen many, mostly overgrown, unused and pointed out as curiosities, but although I was born when the King-Emperor still ruled India [just], the outside privy was not part of my life. I was brought up mostly in Ealing and Surrey and the first house I remember was Edwardian and had two lavatories, one upstairs and the other in the outhouse next to the coal shed. Always cold in winter or summer, we avoided it and my father used it mainly for his 'home-brew' beer and home-made wines. We used to help him collect the elderflowers and berries. I digress. It had a continuous wooden seat in which the central hole section was hinged. A one-seater, I suppose I could call it.

Farm holiday memories in remote mid Wales, or visits to Derbyshire relatives and my grandparents' friends in Lincolnshire and Nottinghamshire were spent trying to avoid using outside privies. That's all very well because in Britain, even in my 1950s boyhood, the flush toilet was everywhere and it was only when one went to villages and farms that universality collapsed. Mind you, the high level cistern flush at the end of its long pipe tended to be a problem. After a few minutes of frantic pulling on the chain a voice would come through the door telling a crimson faced boy the secret of pulling the offending chain just so. My children have had to put up with the inaccurate phrase about always 'pulling the chain' from people of my generation, even though virtually all modern flushes are, as the estate agent's particulars put it, luxury low level, ie a lever on the cistern. This is now ceramic, rather than rusting cast-iron on equally rusty brackets suspended dangerously above one's head like a sword of Damocles.

During my near 20 years of working with historic buildings in Buckinghamshire I have had the opportunity to look into numerous privies, sometimes somewhat gingerly. They have

Privies are about people.

ranged from the grand privies in the Tudor lodgings range at Lord Russell's Chenies to small 'necessary' houses rendered utterly unrecognisable by a dense carapace of choking ivy or chest-high brambles and nettles.

This book examines their immense variety and I am extremely grateful to all those owners who showed me their privies or told me tales and anecdotes about them, many of which are included here. I would particularly like to thank Roger Evans, Buckinghamshire's former Historic Buildings Officer, and Julia Smith, now Milton Keynes' Conservation Officer, for their suggestions of privies for me to look at. My wife, Jill, has endured more privy talk than she could reasonably be expected to hear in normal circumstances but like the rest of my family has been helpful and supportive, once the laughter died down!

I know I have missed many privies and can only apologise if your favourite one is not mentioned. All I can say is that researching this book has been great fun and I am very grateful to the publisher, Nicholas Battle, for commissioning me to write it. Once I overcame the chortles of friends and relations, and had endured endless puns about being up to my neck in it and flushed with success, everyone was most helpful. I hope you enjoy this book as much as I have enjoyed researching and writing it.

MARTIN ANDREW

[1]

GONGFARMERS AND GARDEROBES: THE MEDIEVAL & TUDOR PRIVY

The historian of the privy is beset throughout history by a curious human characteristic: a failure to call a spade a spade. Euphemisms run like a rich seam of ore through our consciousness, the glossary at the back of this book probably merely scraping the surface. So in a medieval or Tudor document, does a 'privy chamber' refer to the owner's innermost room or to his house of easement, in itself a splendidly descriptive name? Is his 'chamber' a privy, is his 'lavatory' a washing place or a privy? We are just as bad nowadays.

We have all, I expect, visited a medieval castle and gazed with horror at the brackish well in the dankest tower basement, or looked into the garderobe with its shute or merely a hole and a sheer drop to the moat. 'Garderobe' of course is the French equivalent of the Norman French word 'wardrobe', still in use in English. So garderobe is as much of a euphemism as privy itself, but it sounds so much more technical, although originally meaning merely the store-room for clothes.

The privies of the Middle Ages that we know about are almost all those of the church and the upper classes. A surprising number survive, some even with their stone seats – which must have been very cold and no doubt led to much rheumatism. Reading the sources, the main impression is of having to choose between enjoying the convenience of a privy attached to or very close to a chamber, and suffering the consequent risk of smells.

In the Middle Ages smells, whether from a privy or elsewhere, were a very real concern for it was thought that smells carried disease. Kings, barons and abbots were particularly troubled by this as a privy or garderobe attached to your privy chamber was as much a status symbol as the 'en-suite' is nowadays.

One of the chambers in the sumptuous lodgings range at Chenies with its Tudor fireplace and doorway leading to the privy.

In monasteries and abbeys designers seemed keen to position the privies or rere-dorter above a stream, which ensured that the effluent was washed away. 'Rere-dorter' is a delicacy in itself for it merely means the back dormitory. These privies, with running water beneath or even in some cases with sluice control to allow scouring, were pretty sophisticated. At Durham Priory 'every seate and particion was of wainscot close of either syde very decent so that one of them [the monks] could not see one another, when they weare in that place.' Each privy in the row had its own little window.

Buckinghamshire's monastic remains are not extensive but there are a few remnants of the provision made for their occupants. At Burnham Abbey, an Augustinian nunnery, the 13th-century rere-dorter survives as the upper floor of an L-shaped wing attached to the former dormitory, while there is also evidence of the infirmary garderobe. Its east wall remains with a small square recess for a lamp. Both privy blocks discharged, it would seem, directly into a moat that predated the abbey. At Notley Abbey, an Augustinian monastery near Long Crendon, there may be a privy chamber in the 16th-century Abbot's Lodging, although the evidence is ambiguous.

Elsewhere in the county nothing significant remains of any monastic buildings in recognisable form, but the plan of Little Marlow Priory was recovered by excavation in 1902. This small Benedictine priory, now under the Edwardian garden village of Abbotsbrook, revealed a rere-dorter over a drainage channel, again an L-shaped building as at Burnham Abbey. The privy pit and garderobe foundations at Bradwell Abbey date from after the dissolution of the monasteries when the chapel they were attached to had become a mere stable!

We have all visited castles and seen the many privies in the thickness of the castle walls. These often discharged into the moat via a stone or timber-boarded shute, the latter having disappeared over time. Occasionally a castle under siege found its house of siege (another circumlocution merely meaning 'seat') or garderobe its Achilles heel. At the apparently impregnable Château Gaillard in Normandy the castle was captured in 1204 by besiegers climbing up the garderobe shutes! The mind positively boggles at this and I pass rapidly on. Many castles had pit privies and complicated arrangements of garderobe towers with several storeys of privies, but I will not go further into this as no castles survive in Buckinghamshire.

Buckinghamshire had royal connections in the Middle Ages. There was a royal residence at Brill, now long gone and whose site was in a field north of the church. Although some refer to it as a palace, it was probably more of a royal hunting lodge for the surrounding royal Forest of Bernwode. In 1248 Henry III, a monarch of considerable fastidiousness, ordered 'a wardrobe and a privy chamber to the same wardrobe' to be constructed at Brill.

There was also a royal residence at Princes Risborough from the 13th-century onwards which centred around the royal stud.

Edward III's son, the Black Prince, was particularly keen and visited often. His interest is perpetuated by the 14th-century addition of 'Princes' to the place-name. Excavations have revealed the plan of much of the manor house, now under The Mount car park near the church. The excavation report concluded that there was evidence of a garderobe attached to what seemed to have been the solar wing.

These are slight evidences, but the other major royal connection in the county is of course Eton College, founded by Henry VI in 1440, and taken from the county in 1974. It was built on the collegiate plan around quadrangles and like most such buildings of the period made provision for the occupants' bodily needs. Sets of rooms had privy or garderobe turrets. These turrets survive on the outer walls of the north and east ranges of the Green Court, but years of change and adaptation mean they no longer have 'innards' in the shape of privies.

No medieval privies survive in Buckinghamshire towns, but we know that in general there was a cavalier disregard of passers-by. Many towns of the period had houses with overhanging latrines that discharged onto the road below. Indeed, in 1321 Ebbegate Street in London was actually blocked completely by waste from the overhanging latrines 'which discharged putridity upon the heads of passers-by'. There were even public lavatories, such as those referred to at Queenhithe in London in 1237 which discharged directly into the river Thames.

Clearing of privy pits was not a pleasant job, particularly as it was usually left until the pit was near full: a consequence of the high labour costs involved. Their capacity seemed enormous and there are regular references in medieval records to clearing away two to five tons of ordure from them. Clearing took many men many days to complete at wages more than twice those of other labourers. Hardly surprising, I think, and there was often the additional labour cost for paying a man to supervise the 'gongfarmers' to ensure they filled the barrels and did not skimp their unsavoury task. The name was derived from 'gong',

Chenies Manor where the privies were in these massive gabled wings set behind the ornate chimneys.

A Chenies Manor privy seat of the 1520s, the oldest surviving in the county.

being an Anglo-Saxon word for privy, and their task to 'fey' or cleanse.

The privy at least provided privacy for thought away from the communal pressures of medieval life. Indeed, it is said that Martin Luther, who was known to suffer from acute constipation, developed the theories that led to the Protestant Reformation during the long hours he spent in the privy tower of his monastery in the years before 1517.

Accordingly, important guests of the aristocracy or Church were provided with privies attached to their chambers and the best examples of these still surviving in Buckinghamshire are those in the lodgings range at Chenies Manor, added by Sir John Russell in the late 1520s. Originally there were at least eight but four now remain, two with the original seats. They had drops or shutes which discharged through arches at ground level and which can be seen in the flower beds. There is evidence for ventilation shafts into the roof space and one privy was later adapted into a hiding place, perhaps during Queen Elizabeth's reign.

The upper classes also had a portable privy, known as a close stool. The advantage of this was that the owner had the convenience of an en-suite without the privy smells, for the close stool could be carried away daily by the servants and the contents disposed of in a pit well away from the house. These portable close stools were known well before the end of the Middle Ages and were often quite elaborate. Henry VIII's, for example, had a padded seat and apparently had some kind of cistern in a separate case.

Non-portable privies were also known as stools and in aristocratic and royal households movable and immovable alike were administered by the splendidly titled Groom of the Stool, or royal lavatory attendant. This position remained a title of honour long after the official had ceased to cleanse and look after the royal privy or close stool. A most curious survival of this medieval circumlocution is found in the medical world of today where the solicitous doctor asks the patient about his 'stools', in this case of course the product rather than the privy, and no doubt most puzzling to those without a firm handle on history.

[2]

CLOSE STOOLS, CHAMBER POTS AND CLOSETS : TOWARDS THE MODERN AGE

In theory the modern era should have begun with the water closet developed by Elizabeth I's godson, the poet Sir John Harington, in the 1590s. However this device, installed in his house near Bath, was regarded as a joke by his contemporaries. It did not resolve the problem of smells or 'noxious vapours', so until the 19th-century development of the 'washdown' bowl with an S-bend trap there was nothing to stop the vapours from the privy pit wafting back into the room and reminding the great and good of their common humanity. Harington's water closet, though, was too far ahead of its time and technology: it merely consisted of a handle lifting a bung at the bottom of the privy. No one turned their attention to correcting its defects in an era of plentiful servants so the period up to about 1750 was the golden age of the close stool for the gentry. The chamber pot had of course been around for years but was, so to speak, not suitable for serious business.

Close stools were often fine pieces of furniture, covered in velvet or satin pinned on by brass-headed nails and studs set in patterns and with elaborately cushioned seats. We can get some idea of their prevalence in Buckinghamshire by looking at probate inventories from the period, that is lists of furniture and fittings drawn up in connection with wills.

Many of the gentry and well-to-do tradesmen such as maltsters had at least one, while innkeepers often had several, one in each of their best letting rooms. For example, in 1699 the innkeeper Edward Marshall at High Wycombe had them in his six best rooms but none for himself or his family, although in 1706

15

Simon Buck, an Eton innkeeper, had only one for his entire inn and that was kept in the wood loft. The upper gentry's close stool numbers were, as might be expected, more numerous than those lower down the social scale: Sir John Borlase had four at Bockmer House in 1699, described as 'close stoole boxes', Robert Dormer of Dorton House had two in 1694 and Sir Thomas Tyrrell of Thornton House also had two in 1671.

By the later 17th-century close stools occur among the inventories of yeomen, craftsmen and smaller tradesmen, such as Henry Eustace, a Bledlow yeoman who had his close stool in the best bedchamber in 1681, or James Blakelock, a laceman from Newport Pagnell who died in 1696.

There are many references to chamber pots in inventories, but it is often unclear whether they are general purpose pots for chambers or rooms, or what we know as chamber pots, 'potties' or 'gazunders': once again we are victims of euphemism-itis. For example, Josias Geary, a gentleman from Chesham who died in 1689, had chamber pots in his four bed chambers, two pots being in pewter. This seems a likely reference to potties, as does that in William Willmott's inventory in 1690: 'In the Chamber at the Staires Head three pewter Chamber potts [and] a close stoole-panne'. In others they are listed in kitchens, which seems a less likely (and hygienic) location.

So as Harington's water closet faded from view, the gentry relied on servant-serviced close stools and privies continued to be built on medieval lines. Towns remained unhygienic with close stools and chamber pots emptied indiscriminately from upstairs windows into the streets, or with privy pits within the houses or immediately adjacent to them. In the country the labourers and peasantry continued to use the countryside as their toilet while farmers and yeomen built privies outside or inside their houses.

A good example of an internal privy from the 1580s survives at Little Loughton Manor House, now within Milton Keynes. On the first floor, it had a drop or shute beside the chimney stack

Chicheley Hall's 1720s house of easement set within the treed Wilderness.

into a pit at the base of the wall.

The majority of privy provision, however, would have been in separate buildings or structures, often of very light construction, but with the benefit of taking unhygienic smells and 'suillage' away from the living quarters. The great weakness of the indoor shute privy or garderobe had always been the difficulty of adequately cleaning the shutes, while the ghastly labour of clearing out the pits meant it was not done frequently enough.

By the mid 18th-century the separate privy building over its pit became the norm outside the confines of towns. Close stools suddenly became very old fashioned. From this time onwards privies survive in increasing numbers, reaching their peak in the late 19th-century. The pit privy dominated the scene until towards the end of the century, after which the bucket privy became the most common, particularly for cottages and farm-houses. The survival rate is high partly because of the use of better, more permanent building materials at this time.

In Buckinghamshire the most impressive privy building from the polite end of society appears to be the one at Chicheley Hall, not far from Newport Pagnell. In the Wilderness north of the canal is an octagonal building that was long thought to be a garden room. It is in the same brick as Sir John Chester's mansion, designed by the Baroque architect Francis Smith and built between 1719 and 1724. 'Wilderness' is something of a misnomer and usually only means a wooded or well treed area with many paths in which the owner and his family and friends would stroll and converse.

This privy building is in a very high quality brick and has a moulded brick cornice. There were box sash windows in the side elevations and there are the remains of a fine three-panel door. The seat has long gone so it is unclear whether it was a one-holer or a two-holer, but the arched recesses at each end might suggest two seats.

It may be that many of the garden temples and buildings in the great landscaped parks of the 18th-century, such as Stowe

Inside Chicheley's elaborate privy. The front beam survives but not the seat.

or West Wycombe Park, originally contained some kind of facility like a close stool. The circuit of the grounds and park could take hours so houses of easement were obviously needed, particularly when one bears in mind the fact that country houses even then had hundreds of visitors every year. Certainly at Stowe the coyly named The Shepherd's Cote on the south walk west of Eleven Acre Lake was a privy, conveniently situated at a point well away from the house. At Cliveden, Giacomo Leoni's drawings of about 1727 for The Blenheim Pavilion at the west end of the park show a water closet, now long gone.

John Wilkes, the Radical hero of the mid 18th century and a member of the notorious Hell-Fire Club, lived at Prebendal House in Aylesbury. He laid out the gardens in the 1750s, and incidentally inveighed against the depredations of visitors who wandered at will through his grounds. In the auction sale particulars of 1764 there is a reference to a privy located, like Chicheley's, in a wooded area.

As one would expect, the 18th century, that great century of the Age of Enlightenment, turned the spotlight of its genius into the dark corners of the privy. At the upper level of society this homed in on the water closet and by the end of the century these were becoming not only far more numerous but also far more effective. Many had been provided for country houses and the town houses of the upper gentry in the early 1700s but had proved unequal to the all-conquering earth closet and pit privy.

However, help was at hand and inventors like the Yorkshireman Joseph Bramah built on the pioneering flushing and valved closet that Alexander Cummings, a watchmaker, patented in 1775. Bramah's version was patented in 1778 and soon became a runaway success, if I might put it thus. The secret of this success lay in preventing smells returning into the privy chamber, usually by the charmingly named 'stink trap'. Once this was successfully achieved the long march of the water closet began, though initially only at the very top of society. A water supply was essential, of course, and this could be piped, pumped or collected in gutters and cisterns. The last two were problematic, for a flushing system dependent on rain water could be inadequate to meet demand in the smelliest part of the year, the summer when rainfall is normally at its lowest.

A Buckinghamshire example of water closet provision in the early 19th century took place at Stowe, where the Dukes of Buckingham installed not only four bathrooms and a shower-room but also nine water closets, one of which was disguised as a cupboard until the door was opened. At a mansion on this scale, while the servants continued to use privies outside, the Duke, his family and guests had conveniences virtually of modern standards.

In towns the spread of water closets was much quicker than in the countryside as piped water was a pre-requisite. By the mid 19th century most middle class homes had water closets and by 1900 few urban developments did not have water closet provision, not necessarily inside the house, of course, but attached. The privy spent the rest of the 20th century retreating to isolated villages and farms. Even in prosperous Buckinghamshire there were villages without running water into the 1960s. Mostly by this time they had Elsan type chemical privies, but in places bucket privies remained in use with no alternative into the 1970s.

Early water closets are of interest and various 19th-century types were installed by progressive farmers. There is a fine example of a two-holer adapted for water, but retaining the hinged lids and seats of the earlier styles in a farm near Marsworth and close to the Hertfordshire border. This is a farmhouse of about 1860 built in yellow stock brick. The privy is at the end of a short walled path from the back door of the house. Beyond the wall is the farm garden and behind the privy a vegetable garden. The privy discharged into a cesspit via earthenware pipes. It is a standard two-holer with one for a child but below the seats are the early conical earthenware ceramic lined bowls

21

A farm near Marsworth has a yellow stock brick wing attached to an out-building at the end of a walled path from the house.

Near Marsworth. Inside is a two-holer with early ceramic bowls piped to a cess pit nearby. The pans, never plumbed, were presumably washed down by buckets of water.

that had a side feed pipe and a drainhole at the bottom of the cone. This example is interesting in that it appears never to have been plumbed! So presumably, as was quite common, it was flushed from a bucket of water kept in the privy building. It is still connected to a working cesspit but there is no smell back draught, thank goodness.

These conical water closet bowls were manufactured all over the country, but there was one maker that I know of in Buckinghamshire, at Akeley near Buckingham. Here the Akeley Pottery turned out drain pipes by the mile and other such products as well as water closet bowls. There are two examples in the Old Gaol Museum in Buckingham, one from a (mostly) demolished toll house on the Tingewick Road.

The other main strand of invention that occupied the minds of inventors was improving the earth closet, again partly in the interest of health and partly to try to eliminate smell. In many

Early glazed earthenware lavatory pans, now in The Old Gaol Museum in Buckingham. The one on the left was made at the Akeley Pottery, near Buckingham.

ways this was parallel to water closet developments without the water. That is to say, much ingenuity and effort went into developing dispensers of earth and ash into the pit or bucket to neutralise odours. Pulling a lever or turning a handle to dispense a measured amount of ash or earth was very much a refinement and removed the earth trowel from the hands of delicate ladies, and there were numerous patented mechanisms and hopper systems evolved. The most celebrated was the Reverend Henry Moule's and examples of this type can still be found in the county. This could be used for ash or earth and, provided the bucket was emptied regularly, was apparently almost odourless. A great improvement over the old pit privies where only the floor and its emptying hatch was between the privy-user and the ordure pit. Enough said, I think.

The best example I found was the one at Mill End Farm, Hambleden, where the privy is in an attached building near the

Mill End Farm, Hambleden. Inside is a fine example of the Rev. Henry Moule's patent ash dispensing closet. Note the pull handle to the left of the seat hole and the intact bucket with its handle.

kitchen on the garden side. It has its own old tile pitched roof and is in brick, as is the rest of the farmhouse. It is a one-holer with a hinged lid. It retains all the mechanism and its pull handle and is a Moules Patent. Although there is a fair amount of rust the system is complete and had the advantage of being independent of any water supply. This example was obviously regarded as something special for the lower part of the walls are lined with salvaged 17th-century panelling and the upper parts are boarded out with tongued-and-grooved planks. Clearly designed for a long and comfortable stay.

I will conclude with an anecdote about Jerome K. Jerome, the author of *Three Men In A Boat*, who lived in Marlow before moving to Marlow Common. He had a privy or, as they were often euphemistically known, a *garden house* at 'Fisherman's Retreat' with a flagpole attached. When he or others went up the garden path they raised the flag, and lowered it when they left. A neat device and no doubt the subject of much raillery.

[3]

PRIVY SURVIVAL

When I started out on this mission I had no real idea how many outside privies survive in Buckinghamshire. I had come across them during the course of my work as a local authority historic buildings advisor and had occasionally been urged to inspect what the new owner had thought to be a small shed. Pulling open the door he would ask me what I thought of that. I would brush away the cobwebs and emerge with an air of authority. That, I would explain, is or rather was a privy. Sometimes there would be the remnants of the seat, which should have given the game away you would have thought, sometimes the front boards and sometimes nothing but an area of unplastered

No. 22 Great Hampden's privy with its little friend.

Inside the seat, the beer barrel cover and even the bucket, all intact.

Around the back there's the bucket hatch and the bucket, complete with its handles and half full of ash.

wall where the woodwork would have been. That was then: this is now. Virtually the day after I started researching for this book I saw my first complete Bucks privy almost by chance.

I was on a site visit to an historic building in Great Hampden village, in the heart of the Chilterns, to discuss an extension to a 17th-century timber-framed house. There, about six metres from the back of the house in splendid isolation stood a one-holer privy. It was built in flint with brick dressings and had an old clay tiled roof. The door could not be opened without moving plants and ornamental logs out of the way. To its left was a child's Wendy House and a rose tree grew picturesquely across the front.

Excitedly I asked if I could move the flower pots out of the way to look inside (I had by now lost interest in the proposed extension to the house). I prised open the door and there was the single-holer intact. Peering through the seat I saw the galvanised bucket half full of ash! The cover for the privy seat was another exciting find: it had been adapted from the top of a barrel from Wheeler's Brewery, according to the lettering on it. Wheeler's had been one of Buckinghamshire's leading breweries, based in High Wycombe five miles to the south.

Outside again, I found the emptying hatch at the rear intact. Had the bucket just been left as it was in the 1960s, perhaps with an extra scattering of ash over its contents, when abandoned in favour of the newly installed indoor flush toilet? I could not believe my luck, finding such a complete privy of such quality almost by chance. The owner and I swapped feeble puns on the lines of being flushed with success and I drove off a contented man. It was a splendid beginning to my fieldwork for this book!

Before discussing the architecture and styles of Buckingham-shire's privies let me introduce you to the range of building materials found in the county, for without this the logic of their use in building the 'necessary houses' will not be clear.

Buckinghamshire is a county without high quality building stone in any quantity. However, usable building stones of varying quality are found and there are clays which were all used for brick making in over a hundred local brick pits. By the mid 19th-century 'foreign' building materials were cheap enough to use even for privies and you can find many roofed in Welsh slate with London stock yellow brick walls. It is important to remember also that privies often used bricks rejected for better quality work and poor timber while the better material was used for the house or cottage nearby: another reason for many disappearing.

Starting in the far north of the county and heading south the geology is, in simplified form: limestone; clay; limestone with some Greensand sandstone; clay, here in brick form and used for mass earth walling, the witchert of the Haddenham area and rather like Devon or Dorset cob; next the chalk hills of the Chilterns which occupy much of the south of the county and provide huge numbers of flints and some chalkstone; and finally along the Thames more clay.

A witchert built privy and walls at Temple Croft in Upton.

Occasionally chalk stone or clunch from the chalk of the Chilterns is mixed in with the flints and even broken bricks and bits of bottle ends were used to bulk up the rubble walling, in short anything to hand. Clay, besides being used for making bricks and witchert was used everywhere to make roof tiles. Thatched roofs also survive on privies.

The material I have not so far mentioned is wood. This is of course a universal building material and is obviously found to some extent in every privy. However, in terms of survival of completely timber-framed privies, the odds are longer. They were usually of light timber with weatherboards nailed over and are particularly vulnerable to rot and demolition either through deliberate act or by neglect. A brick or stone privy can withstand huge amounts of neglect and abuse before collapsing, whereas a timber one, as often as not built in softwood, can be saturated permanently or strangled by a covering of ivy or creeper and disintegrate relatively rapidly. Good maintenance is the key and perhaps the largest concentration of survivors is in the National Trust's West Wycombe village, but others are few and far between.

'Golden Age' privies in Buckinghamshire fall into three sizes: the one-holer, the two-holer and the three-holer. A second key classification is whether the privy is detached, is part of an outbuilding or is built on as an addition.

The main types in Buckinghamshire are the bucket privy and the pit privy. Each has its advantages and disadvantages. Obviously the pit has greater capacity than a bucket, so does not need emptying so often. On the other hand it is rather easier carrying a bucket (at arm's length?) than digging out a pit! It is also much easier to build a bucket privy than a pit one. The pit was usually underneath the seat and the capacity of the pit can be worked out from a typical three-holer: a potential of at least a cubic metre of waste before it needs removal. In fact, I need hardly say, emptying the pit took place far more frequently, but the smells and flies must have been ever-present.

The one-holer is the most common with two-holers and three-holers invariably having one of their number at a lower level for children. Often one of the parents used the adult privy at the same time and quite frequently people remembered this. For example in Brill a lady remembered, as a girl, going on the child's level privy at the same time as her grandmother used the adult one. However, because there is more than one hole in a privy it does not follow that, like Roman garrisons, every hole was used at the same time. It merely gave a choice to suit various bottom sizes. Although one of the people who wrote to me recalled a friend's husband, when a boy, spying on his parents seated side by side on the farm two-holer. Obviously there was less concern with privacy in the past but there would have been etiquettes of acceptability: husband and wife, mother and daughter, father and son acceptable: strangers, teenage boys and girls, etc, not acceptable.

The survival rate of the privy buildings themselves is considerably higher than that of the 'innards', that is the seats, boxes, buckets and fittings. The reason for this is fairly obvious, for once the owner had the luxury of an indoor toilet the privy became redundant. From then on survival is a matter of chance. If it could be utilised as a store or garden shed and it was in the right location it would remain, sometimes with the innards intact but more often, I am afraid, with them removed. A solid concrete floor would replace the earthen one and there you have it: a perfect garden or toolshed. Others survive through being in inaccessible locations and just left to fend for themselves. Often this type retains its innards.

A further refinement is where the privy becomes a store immediately after it falls from use and the innards are buried under old rakes, seed trays, garden wire, bulb racks, sieves, old sacks and anything else, perhaps topped off by children's paddling pools and kiddy trikes! One such took 20 minutes to clear sufficiently

The family two-holer.

so that I could photograph it. Well worth it as it happened, for buried under accumulated years of storage was an intact Moules Patent ash dispensing system.

Thus survival of the innards is very much a matter of chance. Ironically, continued toilet use of a privy building posed a greater threat to the original innards, for updating to a water closet, usually via an Elsan chemical toilet, meant stripping out the interior each time. Occasionally a privy was adapted to flushing but retained the original woodwork, such as that in the old gaol in Buckingham, which as a consequence is still in use.

Privies are to be found all over the county but the pattern of their distribution is interesting. Ownership seems to be the key. Where cottages are tenanted or tied the privies have more or less survived, not necessarily as privies now but as garden stores and sheds. If they have survived until now, the disposal of many estate cottages for sale means their future may be more precarious.

However, no one has enough storage these days so maybe I'm taking an over gloomy view. For example, I found one in Hambleden used to store and restore a classic English motorcycle, another of my interests so I am afraid I was diverted from the privy trail for a few minutes. Another had been converted into a chicken shed with a wire-netting run attached, the hens coming in and out through the former bucket-removing hatch in the privy's back wall. I thought that a marvellous piece of adaptation.

[4]

ESTATE PRIVIES

Estate-built privies mostly date from the later 19th-century and reflect the era of the improving landlord when the living conditions for the labouring poor caused widespread concern. Many of these improvements reflected an enlightened approach for there was no alternative to the privy in the days before universal water mains.

Some of the big and even the not so big landed estates built privies for their tenants at the same time that they built estate cottages. A good example is Sir Henry Acland's Ewelme Estate at Marsh Gibbon which built paired stone cottages throughout the village in the 1880s. They were a great improvement on the near-slum, higgledly-piggledy, tiny cottages of The College,

The Ewelme Estate's 1880s privy/storeshed building for a pair of cottages. The paler door leads into the former privy.

beyond the church, which by the 1880s were an insanitary sink of disease.

Acland also provided a Reading Room for the moral improvement of his tenantry, but more to the point each pair of cottages was provided with an outbuilding, part privy, part store. They were built in local limestone with timber doors and windows and have old tile roofs. Nearly all survive, although I understand none retain their privies.

In the north of the county Lord Carrington's Gayhurst Estate built pairs of brick cottages, again in the fashionable Tudor style beloved of Victorian estate surveyors as redolent of Merrie England. The cottages have the intersecting 'C' motif of the Carringtons set in stone panels. The privies are in the far outer corner of each pair, with store-sheds occupying the parts nearest the house. Most of these cottages were improved in the 1950s with lean-to extensions to accommodate bathrooms and toilets so the privies have been redundant for years. A good example of the outbuilding/privy block is the pair at Bunsty Farm Cottages on the Hanslope Road.

Many cottage privies survive on other estates, such as the Hambleden Estate where for instance a block of three privies once serving three cottages at Mill End are now used as sheds. Many estate privies here were in use until the 1950s, for example one until 1956. The estate sent a 'lavender cart' around to collect the privy waste. This cart was kept in a shed next to the blacksmith's forge in the centre of Hambleden village, now a garage, and one suspects that its perfumes severely affected the summer atmosphere of the village.

Further along the Thames towards Medmenham, Westfield Cottages retain their privy blocks. These were six pairs of cottages built for Robert Hudson, the soap baron who built Danesfield House. Each has a relief over the front door in local glazed pottery showing farmwork for a month of the year. The cottages and their privies/stores, also in pairs behind the cottages, were designed in about 1900 by W.H. Romaine-Walker,

Architect Romaine-Walker's 1900 Arts and Crafts Style privies at Westfield Cottages, Medmenham, for the Danesfield estate.

one of the leading architects of his day who also designed Danesfield House itself. They have an Arts-and-Crafts feel with tiled roofs to them.

At Chenies the Dukes of Bedford built a model village around the village green in two phases. The first, in simpler style, has 1820s datestones, each pair originally with a privy/store block behind. The second was a more picturesque phase in a Tudorish style with leaded casements and elaborate chimneys. These have datestones with the Bedford badge and are mostly dated 1849. Each pair or group of three (you could not call such picturesque artfulness a terrace) had a tile-roofed brick range close to their backs which included a privy, a store and a central laundry block. According to the occupants to whom I spoke no innards survive, which is a shame as they are such well dated examples.

There were many other improving landlords in Buckinghamshire – the Dashwood Estate in West Wycombe, the Wyndhams of Tythrop, the Hampden Estate at Great and Little Hampden, the Tyrwhitt-Drakes at Amersham, Lord Chesham at Latimer and the Rothschilds just about everywhere across the centre of the county, including Mentmore, Waddesdon and Upper Winchendon. They are just a few of those who improved the lot of their tenantry in the Victorian age.

The landlords were also not idle in improving the lot of their tenants in existing cottages and farms. The Dashwood Estate in West Wycombe village, for instance, built a large number of timber-framed and weather-boarded privy/store blocks for their tenants. These have tiled roofs and the boards in the gables are drilled with holes to provide ventilation. There are several behind Crown Court in the High Street, for example, where there is also a single-holer small weatherboarded privy and a pair built in brick in the 1940s to the orders of Captain J.B. Hill, the Dashwoods' agent. Some are still in use, but with water closets, while others are now sheds. The estate also built brick, and brick and flint privies in the village, as at Lacemakers and Rose Cottages at the west end of the High Street. The Estate

West Wycombe: Brick and flint and tiled roofed privies off the High Street.

A triple privy at The Closes, Hardwick, one per cottage.

was relatively unusual in building so many privies in timber with weatherboarded elevations.

Others are found at Great Hampden, and there is one at Gate Cottage in Horsenden built for Mrs Leonard Jaques, the lady of the manor, in about 1890 as part of her programme of estate improvements. Built in brick with a tiled roof and now without innards, it is used as a garden store but retains its rear bucket hatch. Other smaller landlords and estates provided privy blocks when necessary. In Hardwick, The Closes, a 17th-century farmhouse subdivided into three cottages after 1778, was provided with a block of three privies in brick with a slate roof in the 1890s.

The village of Lane End near High Wycombe still retains a large number of privies and evidence of where cesspits and pits were located. This is a curious village where houses from the 1860s to 1880s of almost urban quality line the main through road, including a former temperance hotel. Even the cottages have an urban quality, built in tall terraces or pairs. Many privies survive and the local historian Raymond Harris showed me some and told me he had been born and brought up in The Old Bakehouse which had an outside privy.

'I can remember finding my way down the garden path carrying a candle stick, with one hand cupped round the candle itself to prevent the wind extinguishing the flame,' he recalled. 'There are several of these brick edifices still to be found in our village. Externally they have not changed, but no doubt they are now used for a variety of different purposes. They were not restricted to any one design, to enable the pail to be removed for emptying some had lift-up seats, others a trap door on the outside. Some were built in rows and had a communal pit along the rear.

'I once knew one that had two seats, one at a lower level presumably for the benefit of children. My mother used to recount an amusing story of one occasion when the builder's apprentice was made to sit on the seat while the outline of his bare bottom was marked in pencil on the uncut wood.

Lane End: the privy and store range across a small yard at Church Cottages. Note the fish-scale roof tiles above the privies.

41

Wing: pairs of privies alternate with pairs of store sheds for Albert Terrace of 1882.

'The local pubs had gents-only ones, even more basic. A three-sided brick enclosure open to the sky, with no more than an iron drain in the floor. I know of one that still exists except that two of the walls have been demolished, but the grating is still in the floor. Where the discharge point is or was is anybody's guess.' At the Clayton Arms pub, incidentally, an old boy from Cressex had spent such a long time in the privy over the years that his ashes were scattered outside it.

Industrial employers also built cottages for their employees and in the later 19th-century provided them with privies. A dated example in Wing will illustrate this quite well. Albert Terrace, Nos 51 to 57 Littleworth, is a brick terrace of four cottages with an 1882 date plaque. They were built by the owner of the local brickyard for his workers, and indeed on the opposite side of the road is a pond which is the site of one of his brick pits. They have a small communal yard at the rear (no gardens) in which pairs of corrugated-iron roofed privies alternate with paired

At Gayhurst, William Burges's vast and elaborate Servants Lavatory for Lord Carrington is watched over by Cerberus, the guard dog of Hades and sewers. A privy to end all privies.

43

store-sheds. They were in use until 1951 as bucket privies after which they were converted to flushing toilets. Mrs Sawyer, one of the residents, can remember using the bucket privy behind her cottage. Naturally the bricks were made in the landlord's brick pit and, unsurprisingly, look like 'seconds'.

At Buckingham the cottages built by the railway company around 1900 have outlasted the station itself. A terrace of six cottages for railway workers were provided with pairs of privies backing onto an alley that runs behind the rear gardens. They were unusual architecturally in having an almost flat concrete slab roof. No innards survive.

Before leaving the estate-built privy I must round off with the mother and father of them all – The Servants Lavatory at Gayhurst House. This extraordinary building was designed by William Burges, the architect of Cardiff Castle and Knightshayes Court in Devon, and built in 1859-1860 for the somewhat eccentric Lord Carrington. It is a circular version of the celebrated medieval Abbot's Kitchen at Glastonbury Abbey, built in rubblestone with finer stone used for dressings. The conical tiled roof is surmounted by a statue of the three-headed dog Cerberus, the dog that guarded the entrance to Hades or the underworld in Greek mythology. Due to this connection Cerberus was associated with drains, sewers and human waste, hence his presence here. Originally the statue had red glass eyes as well, presumably to scare away diseases. Internally, the plan seems to have copied that of the 14th-century Archbishop's Palace at Southwell in Nottinghamshire with privies distributed around a central column. Now the building has been converted into a house, but the exterior is little altered. A fitting climax to the story of the estate privy!

[5]

FARMERS AND COTTAGERS

Farmhouses undoubtedly offer the most variety in privy sizes and types, ranging from three-holers downwards for the family, to provision for farm workers.

The surviving three-holer is an elusive beast in Buckinghamshire. I came across former ones, now outbuildings, and people remembered them from farms long demolished, but the only complete one I found was in Brill. The owner, who was told the privies were in use in the 1940s, had lovingly restored its three seats, one a lower level child's privy, and even more impressively had excavated the pit and restored the opening flaps in the floor which gave access to it. He had even added a light within the pit, which is about 5 feet deep.

Also in Brill, Red House in Church Street has a delightful brick-built privy which is set into a garden wall of local limestone. The front is flush with the wall and the privy body lies beyond the wall, now a salient into the garden of the modern house next door. It has a pitched old tile roof and is charmingly creeper clad which almost conceals the window. The owner tells me it was a three-holer, but it is now a useful garden shed with a concrete floor.

Other three-holers whose trail I came across included Bedgrove Farm on the outskirts of Aylesbury: no chance of seeing that bucket three-holer now as its site lies under a 1960s housing estate. At Widmere Farm, north of Marlow, the building has survived as an outside lavatory with a single water closet replacing the three-holer. It was a pit privy in a classic position at the end of a hedged walk from the back door. Behind a wall at the rear was its pit, in effect a corner of the (still very active) vegetable garden. The owner's sister, the Marlow historian Rachel Brown, recalled the superb vegetables they had when children

A beautifully restored three-holer in Brill. Note the pit hatch in the foreground.

from this human-manured garden.

At Brook Farm, Milton Keynes village, the brick-built three-holer was given some pretensions architecturally and is doubly interesting for a latrine was made for the farm workers in the gap between it and an adjacent outbuilding.

Others that survive as buildings include that at The Limes Farm at Upper Winchendon where the successor to the three-holer, now a limestone rubble and tile-roofed garden shed, was built as a lean-to further along the house. There was a pit three-holer at West Park Farm, Wing, and a lean-to roofed one near the kitchen door, now a store shed, at Bencombe Farm, near Marlow.

Two-holers at farms are numerous and the survival rate some-what better. A most interesting example is at Manor Farm Cottages, Nos 7-9 The Green at Little Loughton, formerly a 16th- and 17th-century farmhouse but divided into two cottages later and provided with a pair of back-to-back two-holers, one adult

Manor Farm Cottages, Loughton: the second intact privy I visited: a won-derfully complete pair of two-holers.

Manor Farm Cottages, Loughton: I cleared away the rubbish to reveal the child's seat and lid. An exciting moment for me and the owner.

and one child seat in each. Built in brick in the later 19th-century, they share a slate roof with doors either side of the party wall. Whitewashed walls and circular privy seats with lift-off covers complete the picture and happily a couple of the buckets remain in situ.

At Castle Farm, Lavendon, the privy, built in stone and with a thatched roof, was also a back-to-back with one accessed from the walled garden and the other from the fields. There is a substantial hatch for raking out the pit (lovely job).

At Old Arngrove Farm, near Boarstall, the farmer built a brick outhouse in the 1880s for his farm workers with a pair of back-to-back two-holers. Operational until after the Second World War, apparently one two-holer was for men and the other for women. It is quite close to the farmhouse and I suspect the segregation relates to the war when Land Army girls were there, for one privy pair was entered from the farmhouse garden and the other from the farm side.

At Castle Farm, Lavendon, a two-holer entered from the walled garden and a one-holer entered from the field side. Note the one intact pit emptying hatch and a blocked one nearby.

Vi Cowley, one of my correspondents, recalled her Land Army days near Lillingstone Lovell. She lived at Glebe Farm and worked at Pittams Farm, now Lovell Wood Farm. The privies have long gone but her memories have not: 'My friend Kitty and I had our meals with a farm worker and his family of six males, three females and us two land girls, and one bucket lavatory! All the men folk walked into the woods every morning carrying a sheet of newspaper, we females used the bucket. At Glebe Farm I lived with two sisters, both single and in their late sixties. They had a double seated bucket lavatory, for mother and child, one hole bigger than the other.'

Moving on to single-holers, I particularly like the one at Dad Brook Farm, Cuddington, which is square-ish and built in witchert, the earth walling material common in a band across the middle of the county, with a pyramidal thatched roof. A similar witchert one is at Temple Croft, a small farm near

At Dad Brook Farm, Cuddington, a fine thatched privy built in witchert (local cob) on a stone plinth or, locally, 'grumplings'.

Dinton. There was much repair necessary in 1985 when it was 'in collision with a tractor'.

Many farms, of course, had more than one privy and Dock Farm at Meadle, near Princes Risborough is a good example. The house is 17th-century and had two one-holers, one of which survives as a lean-to between the house gable and an out-building. When I visited the farm the owner, Colin Barry-Smith, said he had some old bits of timber from the privy in a shed and these turned out to be the complete seat and circular lid. He also produced a long-handled implement with a circular bowl in iron. This looked to me like a 'jut' or privy pit emptying implement. Presumably it survived from a pit privy on the farm, but both remaining ones had been bucket types.

One-holers are found, in varying states of decay, all over the county. For example, the middle of the county at Marsh Gibbon, Cromwell House, a former farmhouse in the village, has a local rubblestone and old tile-roofed privy. It is almost

At Dock Farm, Meadle, Colin Barry-Smith displays his privy emptying 'jut' and his next restoration project: the privy seat.

51

A thatched and painted brick privy at The Hollow Tree Restaurant, Stoke Goldington, backs onto a stream and can be seen from the road.

A delightful one-holer from the eastern end of the county: Littlelands at Coleshill.

hidden by ivy, with the privy front boards and the bucket intact in its cobwebbed interior. It is curiously situated in line with the house front so that any passers-by could see comings and goings. In the 1920s a common brick replacement was built opposite the back door and the privy reduced to woodshed status.

To round off this farmhouse section, there is an interesting double privy shared by Cozens Holding and Rest Awhile in Owlswick, near Princes Risborough. Here two small farms shared a pair of one-holers, side by side under a single old tile roof and built in mellow local brick, but entered from doors in the gardens of each farm. Rest Awhile is dated 1756, and the contemporary privies each have a hinged flap.

Small privies were often built for cottages by the tenants themselves, often copyholders or life tenants as well as owners and smallholders. These are almost invariably one-holers and occur all over the county. They include one at Wield Cottage in Townside, Haddenham, which is still in use as it was modernised by having a water closet installed. At Walnut Tree Cottage in Longwick there is a good brick one-holer and at Clematis Cottage, South End, in Turville parish, there is a well-restored timber-framed and weatherboarded privy.

At 49 High Street, Amersham, now the Amersham Museum, there is a paired privy at the end of the long narrow garden, one for No 49, the other for Vine Cottage, No 47, next door. In brick and tile, its innards have gone, although the seat support battens remain. These small privies come in all styles and all materials, but the survival of their innards is relatively rare, and these few examples will suffice. Many of you will know of other examples and this book is not intended to be an exhaustive gazetteer, so you, dear reader can fill in the gaps!

Cozens Holding, Owlswick: inside the seat and lid are intact.

At Amersham Museum, located in a rescued medieval hall house, you can 'go up the garden path', but the privy, well repaired, is now only a store shed.

[6]

TOWNEES AND OTHER PRIVIES

There was a great deal of speculative building for rent in the 19th-century, which was either provided with outside privies from the start or had them added as 'improvements', no doubt with a suitable adjustment to the rent. Many of these were in towns and survive in numbers, although mostly converted to outside stores, often festooned with padlocks. Much of what I am going to describe can be duplicated in every town in the county, depending on the extent of 20th-century redevelopment of course. Little of old Slough, for example, survives.

In Olney, Nos 1 to 8 Bridge Street date from about 1840. There is a communal pathway along the rear with gardens beyond, in which were three pairs of privies and single ones for the end houses. Now only a pair and the single privy for No 8 survive. They are in brick with slate roofs and are surprisingly narrow with the doors discreetly facing up the garden. The drawback of this arrangement would be that no one would know whether the privy was occupied until they rattled the door. Still, I think it preferable to all the privy doors opening onto the walkway.

Less grand but still in Olney, Nos 5 to 9 Weston Road, a mid 19th century terrace of brick and slate roofed cottages, had a privy block built soon after 1900 using common brick and roofed in corrugated-iron. Above the doors are vents formed by leaving gaps between bricks and the doors have ornamentally cut tops which also helped in ventilation. The block is at right angles to the road and the occupants of Nos 5 and 7 would have had to pass No 9 to get to their privy. Needless to say they are no longer in use, although one retains a flushing toilet, a later modernisation.

Further south quite a few privy buildings survive in Chesham,

One of the privies at the back of Nos 1 to 8 Bridge Street, Olney.

such as those near and behind Nos 4 to 9 Bury Lane, two built against the high wall surrounding the rectory as lean-tos with their doors onto the lane and their cottages on the other side of the lane. To use them the tenant of this yard terrace had to cross the lane to get to his privy where, built on the lane verge, he had presumably literally established squatter's rights!

In Wendover there are quite a few 19th century privies surviving. The two behind No 5 Pound Street, a 17th century timber-framed house, can be seen from the road. Curiously one is in brick and tile, the other in brick and slate, and it is clear that the house was once sub-divided and a privy built for each at different times. Wendover also has a terrace of early 19th century cottages built in a yard off Back Street, grandly called Chandos Place, which like most such speculative cottages for rent have virtually no yard behind them but just enough room for privies. However, only a couple of the privies survive and are now water closets.

These sort of privies were added to small town developments all over the county but their survival rate is relatively low. Many of these yard cottages, crammed into every spare bit of land behind frontage houses, are now modernised into young professionals' starter homes: quite a change from their origins as cheap housing for rent for the very poorest townspeople. Very few privies survive this modernisation.

Outside privies continued to be built for rented housing well into the 20th-century, rather than lose space inside and have the expense of plumbing. A good example is a block of three behind Nos 50 to 54 Bell Street in Princes Risborough, built in common brick with corrugated-iron roofs. Dating from the 1920s, they were provided with flushing toilets from the start and in a way represent the end of a tradition.

Mercifully, the indoor privy is a rarity, for the farmer, his labourers and the town dweller had no wish, normally, to share their living quarters with the earth closet or privy. In rural areas

The end of a tradition: a 1920s block of three lavatories behind Nos 50 to 54 Bell Street, Princes Risborough.

you could, in any case, always nip out for a 'country one', that is a visit to a countryside hedge or wood where a bunch of bracken, straw, grass, or dock leaves replaced the squares of cut up *Daily Sketch*.

I only came across one indoor privy of traditional type, that is without a water supply, and that has now mercifully gone. A fine timber-framed cottage complete with jettying at No 2 Bell Walk, Winslow, had one beside the stairs in the kitchen until less than two years ago. It was a single holer with a ceramic or enamel pan which was flushed by a bucket of water. The privy had little foot room between its front boards and the shed-type door, and was painted sky blue and canary yellow. Many will recall the outside, where the owner had painted the brickwork and the timbers in very bright colours. It was something of a local landmark and owned by a, literally, colourful eccentric, known locally as Mad Arthur.

This sort of thing is of course unusual, but many indoor

Mad Arthur's indoor privy at No. 2 Bell Walk, Winslow, in some sort of use until the 1990s.

lavatories of more traditional type have been enriched – such as one in London Road, High Wycombe, where a verger's chair was converted into a lavatory.

Moving on to more conventional provision, Nonconformist chapels and meeting houses usually made adequate provision for visiting ministers and preachers who may have travelled some way to preach. Dissenters seem always to have been more down to earth in such matters. It is only in the last few years that the Church of England appears to have noticed its clergy's bodily functions, although a quick dash to the vicarage was presumably considered the normal option. At Chenies in the 1770s the Particular Baptists provided a privy for their new chapel. It is shown on the 1779 Trust Deed, illustrated by Christopher Stell in his *Non-Conformist Chapels and Meeting Houses: Buckinghamshire*. Labelled 'A Privy', it is behind a stable in the far corner of the site. The stable survives, so it can be precisely dated, but of the privy there is no trace. However, its site is lower than the stable and occupied by graves. Is it possible that the pit of the privy now contains Baptist worthies awaiting the Resurrection?

At Cuddington there is an even more poignant relic. This village's Baptist chapel of 1831 was built in witchert, the local earth wall technique, and collapsed a couple of years ago, leaving only the brick store and part of the privy standing. The graveyard remains with an ivy clad ruin and the later improvement of the ceramic flushing lavatory pan sitting in the open, its west wall having been that of the collapsed chapel. The total reverse of the Chenies example, the spiritual provision has gone, leaving only the base bodily provision as an incongruous memorial.

Almshouses are another class of building in which privy provision came pretty late. For example, the Ravenstone Almshouses north of the church were founded by Heneage Finch, Earl of Nottingham, by 1682. In this stone village the two ranges of six one-up, one-down almshouses were built in fashionable and expensive brick, but without privies, which at that time were only for the upper classes and the top ranks of farmers. They had to wait until the mid 19th-century when two privies were provided by the trustees, one per six cottages. In brick and slate, the earlier boundary wall was raised behind each to form a coped parapet. An occupant told me they had not been used since indoor toilets were provided and are now garden sheds.

Buckingham has a picturesque former gaol in the form of a mock castle, built in 1748 with an exercise yard and two storeys of cells. In the yard a stone-built privy was provided in the angle of two walls with a lean-to tiled roof. It probably dates from about 1840 when the even more castle-like Gaoler's House was added. A timber box privy with a hinged lid, now all much restored, was adapted early this century to a high level cistern flush type, but the box remains. It is notable, of course, that when the prisoners were provided with a privy not many of their contemporaries had them at their dwellings: rather like complaints in the saloon bar about prisoners having television nowadays.

Mains water spelt the death knell of the outside toilet, as much as it did the yard pump or the pump in the kitchen. The 20th-century has seen a steady and complete erosion of self-sufficiency, whether in the water supply from the well, or the oil lamp, the vegetable garden, the log fire and range and even the coal fire. Nowadays no one goes up their garden path to the privy, leaving its door open to chat to the pig in the pen next door, fattening up on scraps until its slaughter to provide meat for the self-sufficient cottager, as remembered by one girl from her childhood near the Bedfordshire border.

Many older people told me how relieved they were that they no longer had to go out in all weathers up the garden path, probably under the eye of their neighbours as their torch beam

At Buckingham Gaol, built in 1748, a privy was eventually provided in the exercise yard in about 1840. It is now converted to a high cistern flusher.

weaved through the night. Most of the people I spoke to had a curious blend of nostalgia in that they were in a way proud of having lived in hardship but pleased that they no longer had to, if you see what I mean. Dislike of the privy at night was virtually universal and no man expressed regret at the loss of the job of emptying the privy bucket or the pit!

[7]

BUCKINGHAMSHIRE MEMORIES

I set off collecting memories for this book full of hope that I would be able to link surviving privies to their users, or at least some of them. This turned out to be surprisingly difficult in Buckinghamshire, due partly to its great mobility of population over the last 50 years or so and to the county's wealth in comparison with other parts of the country.

One thing that became clear was that a surprising number of privies remained in use until well after the Second World War. In many cases mains water did not reach villages until the 1950s, for example Akeley, near Buckingham, in 1957 and Lillingstone Lovell not until the early 1960s. Fortunately many privies survived intact or were converted into sheds and stores but of their users there is rarely a trace. However, the memories linger on. Most of the people who wrote to me or spoke to me were happy to share their memories and I only regret that it is not possible here to include all the reminiscences that they were kind enough to send.

Some were even pleased that they had demolished the privy, on occasion mere months before I spoke to them. There was one elderly lady living on her own at the end of a track off Hawridge Common on the chalk plateau above Chesham. She told me with some glee that she had had it knocked down a few months earlier because she was fed up with seeing such a reminder of her past. In any case why should I want to know about such things. They were best forgotten.

The thing that did surprise me somewhat was that I was welcomed wherever I went. I had feared that a strange man knocking on the door asking to see a privy would be greeted with at best suspicion and at worst by reaching for the telephone to call the police. In fact, nobody was hostile or refused to show me their privy, although one or two did mutter about me wasting my time. In general people were delighted that someone was taking an interest and were proud of their privies. It seems that the privy exercises a fascination for all people, being a form of local history to which we can all relate and one that is not too remote.

Obviously people remembered the type of privy they had, and their memories sounded loud and clear their dislike of the lack of privacy, in some cases even after half a century or more. Everyone could see you trudging up the garden to the single privy or the block of two or three serving a row of cottages and, of course, there was little or no aural privacy.

Mrs Hetty Boddy remembers her pre-First World War child-hood in a terrace of three cottages in One Pin Lane in Hedger-ley. A double privy was shared by three families, a total of 20 people. 'The loo was past the three cottages across a bit of yard, then down another garden, where there was twin loos with wooden seats and wall between the two. They had galvanised buckets which had to be emptied and ashes to be shaken over the contents.'

In the middle of the county May Atkins, as she then was, recalls her childhood in Botolph Claydon in similar circum-stances. 'We lived in the middle house of three, up the garden was a block of three loos, and we had the middle one. They was quite smelly. There was a big bucket and a wooden seat to sit on. When the bucket was full it had to be taken down the garden and emptied. There was no such thing as toilet rolls. You had to cut the daily paper into squares, thread it on some string and hang it on the wall.'

Mrs Margaret Johnson of Latimer in the south of the county has many memories of interest. 'What a coincidence,' she wrote. 'I had been comparing notes with another lady on the joys of "out-door loos" when I saw your letter.

West Wycombe: a weatherboarded one-holer down the garden path.

'I remember as a child we had a wooden box-shaped earth closet with a bucket placed in a strategic position. Everyone worked on Lord Chesham's estate [at Latimer], so a person came round and emptied the loo, and there was a shed where it was left to settle, and we children were dared to go near there. In the mid 1950s the estate was sold, but my parents didn't purchase their house until the early sixties, so we still had an outside loo, though it had been updated to an Elsan type by then, and Dad used to dig a hole in the garden and empty the contents, but always waited until it went dark.'

Mrs Allen of Winslow recalls three different outside lavatories. 'My gran's was a brick affair at the bottom of the yard, it had a window, no lock, but a door. A round basin and a wooden lid on hinges which pulled up. It was flushed with water from the tub in the yard or the weekly soap suds.

'My mother's was much more posh: a brick-built affair in the coal barn with its own door, no lock so we whistled, but with a cistern much like ones today. But it froze up in winter.

'My own lav when I first got married was the gem of them all. No light. It was in the coal barn. A dirt floor and nine barns and lavs in a long row. In the corner a square box (the wooden box), the lid did not lift up. It had to be flushed with water in a bucket. Four bricks left out of the top, for fresh air. No window. The hell-hole was not an experience I would wish my grandchildren to endure.'

On a more cheerful note, Mrs S. Macleod writes. 'The lav was situated just through the shed and was a back to back with next door. It was sited just under a lilac tree which made it quite fragrant and picturesque in Spring! The neighbours kept an aviary next door and the birds were always chirping.'

Of course, in those days toilet paper was not common and in any case, in my boyhood, only the unyielding Bronco or similar hard

Newspaper pieces on a string: a restored privy at the Chiltern Open Air Museum, Chalfont St. Peter.

non-absorbent material was available. Nowadays we have soft tissue but our forefathers had already discovered newspaper recycling long before our 'green' age.

Raymond Harris of Lane End recalls that: 'Loo roll holders were not a usual requirement, all that was needed was a rusty nail on which to hang squares of newspaper threaded on a length of string. Fortunately the ink used to print *The Bucks Free Press* in those days was of a more durable nature than what is used at the present time.'

Mrs Margaret Johnson of Latimer told me: 'Then there was the toilet paper, small squares of newspaper, a skewer driven through the corner, threaded on string. You always found that you started reading, but never found the end of the article. Wouldn't like it now as the print comes off.'

Similarly Mrs Eileen Hudson remembers life in her terraced cottage in Wraysbury, today in Berkshire, built in 1880 but now replaced by 'nice new houses'. There were five privies in a row to serve the cottages on The Green and she writes: 'Another pastime was reading the little squares of newspaper which had previously been cut up, put onto a string. No toilet paper available at that time (wartime). You would get interested in an article only to find the next piece didn't run in sequence so you never had the end of the story.'

Mr Aldridge who lived in Wycombe Lane, Wooburn Green, as a boy remembers that: 'It was my mother's job to cut the *Daily Mirror* into four sections and dad would nail it on a post: the *Daily Mirror* was the most popular newspaper in those days.' It is not clear whether Mr Aldridge means it was most popular as a newspaper or for its wiping qualities and absorbency!

Mrs S. Macleod of Frieth recalls: 'Sitting indoors and tearing squares of newspaper to hang on the string in the lav. It took ages and we kept finding interesting news. I seem to remember the *Daily Sketch* as a favourite.'

Clearing out privy pits, emptying bucket privies or filling

The bucket hatch and bucket: an example from Loughton.

cesspits are other matters that remain in the memory. 'Dad had the job of emptying the lav every week and we had to stay indoors,' recalls Mrs Mcleod of Frieth. 'Mum remembers she had to empty it one week and says it was one of the worst experiences of her life! (Mind you we did have a wonderful vegetable garden - organic gardening is nothing new!)'

In almost identical terms Mr Aldridge of Wooburn Green recalls that his loo 'was a bucket which my father emptied every week and we had a wonderful crop of vegetables. You could tell when the buckets were emptied as all the neighbours had lanterns out to dig the holes. Talk about the Good Old Days!'

Raymond Harris of Lane End gave much useful information on emptying. 'The communal pit along the rear (of the privies) had to be emptied by the use of a long-handled bucket-shaped ladle known as a "jut". For obvious reasons this operation was usually carried out at night. Maybe this was the origin of the name "night-soil".

'The coming of mains water (to the village) made flush toilets possible but it was some time before the main sewer reached the village. Until then the only alternative was a cesspool in the garden, or in some cases a septic tank. The cesspool had to be periodically emptied with the aid of tankers provided by the local council. Once again a procedure not very popular with the neighbours, the operator was usually referred to as "Lavender Jim".'

Mrs Eileen Hudson added more information on life in Wraysbury. 'Once a week the long wooden seat (of the privy) had to be scrubbed with soda and the floor washed and whitened, with Izal disinfectant put in the bucket.

'Also once a week two men came to empty the buckets into the cesspit, then the cesspit was emptied once a month by lorry. It wasn't a very pleasant smell.'

Phyllis Peverill recalls moving to a village near Tingewick at the start of the Second World War from Oxfordshire, where her family had had the luxury of a single privy all to themselves. In Buckinghamshire, where they shared a double privy with the next door family, she recalls: 'One of the hardest things was in the war when there were no men at home to dig the hole in the garden to bury it, especially in winter.'

Actually that sounds remarkably like camping in tents and trudging through the pines to the ablution blocks, so it is not a thing of the past! My family's caravanning holidays in the 1950s involved my father digging a pit upon arrival at the site, tipping the Elsan contents into it periodically and then filling the pit in at the end of the two weeks. I suppose it gave me an insight into the past but I found it unpleasant. My brother and I were 'allowed' to help. Even then it was always the man's job: sensible women, eh?

One of the most striking aspects of the memories I collected was the children's fear of going to the privy, particularly at night.

Mrs Boddy of Hedgerley wrote: 'Oh, how we children used to

be scared if we wanted to go after dark as there was no lighting, just the road to go along and just hoping we didn't have to wait for somebody else to come out as they served all three cottages.

'My dad used to go up there and smoke his pipe. It wasn't so bad in the summer, but when the snow was on the ground or pouring with rain, well, if you was forced to go in the dark, you had to have a torch or a candle.'

Mrs Peverill who lived in a village near Tingewick wrote and wondered: 'How many people would one find now going up the garden in the night with a flashlight or candle with their mac on and an umbrella and wellies?

'We never had anything elaborate, and only had to go across the dark yard, where a part of the shed was partitioned off, and there was also a wooden screen round the door, but even that was bad enough on a wet or cold night. The other thing in the memory is the smell, particularly on warm days. How lucky we are now.'

Mrs Brenda King who lived in the last cottage in a row of four in Botley Road, Chesham recalls: 'The privy was situated in an old wooden shed with a corrugated iron roof and it stood immediately under a large holly tree. As a child I was terrified by the noises on the roof and used to try to avoid using it for as long as possible but my mother would make me "go" when she thought it necessary. In vain did my father try to explain to me that the noises on the roof were made by birds, berries falling from the tree or branches or leaves scratching on the metal when it was windy. I was convinced some nameless thing prowled there waiting to pounce on me when I emerged.'

Eileen Hudson of Wraysbury vividly recalls her fears of going down the garden path to the distant privy at night. 'The thing I hated most was having to go down there late at night. Armed with only a torch I would creep quietly down the path but when getting to our lav I used to cough and bang about in case a cat or rats were in there (a large gap was under the door). Nearby our neighbour kept rabbits so you could hear them scratching about. All very frightening to a child, you could hear your own heart thumping.

'One rainy night I remember sitting there. Suddenly I heard this commotion on the roof where a cat was trying to get to an owl's nest in the fir tree which had babies in. I think the whole of the village must have heard me screaming.'

Mrs Macleod of Frieth had a privy beyond an outbuilding. 'I can remember taking a torch – which always seemed to be on the blink when it was my turn to use it – and picking my way through the terrors of the shed and all the shapes thrown up by the torchlight and then sitting there and hearing the branches tapping against the door and roof.'

Mr Aldridge of Wooburn Green had a different source of terror. 'Our loo was at the top of the garden approximately twelve feet from the railway line and if you happened to be sitting in comfort and you heard the train whistle either from Wooburn or Loudwater you quickly cut things short and made a quick exit, mainly being scared of the train thundering by.'

Modernization to a flushing outside toilet was not always the panacea everyone hoped, as Mrs Brenda King of Chesham recalled. 'In 1938 the local council came to my rescue and condemned the cottages unless the landlord agreed to modernise. This he did. Botley House, the large house just down the road was also renovating at the same time so he bought a job lot of old fittings from there and we all got a "new" sink and a cold water tap (although ours was labelled HOT) and a drain. We also got a water closet but it was still in the garden. It was, however, much nearer to the back door. It was built of brick and had a tiled roof so the noises were gone but a new terror emerged. I was and still am afraid of spiders and the new toilet had white-washed walls thus making these creatures much more visible. I decided that I couldn't win!

'My father was very glad to get rid of the job of coping with the bucket but this privy presented a new problem. How to

A privy from my village: partly buried beneath Parthenocissus, the privy at Wield Cottage, Townside, Haddenham, has been converted to a flush lavatory.

keep it free from freezing in the winter? The one sure solution seemed to be that when a particularly severe period of weather was expected the water had to be turned off and we had to flush our new toilet with a bucket! This toilet was in use until 1970 when the cottages were eventually demolished.'

Many people wrote to tell me of amusing incidents or embarrassments. Mrs Phyllis Peverill, for instance, recalls her neighbour in a village near Tingewick. 'Not only were the houses joined but also the toilets were joined at the top of a long garden. Sometimes the neighbour arrived to hers while you were in yours and it was often quite funny. She used to talk to herself.

'She would grunt and strain then say, "Oh, that's better". At times the sound of her passing wind was quite funny, at times musical. She would then open [the privy] door and talk to her chickens and say, "Come on my little 'ens, lay me some heggs".

'In winter you needed wellingtons on to get up there. One always hoped not to have to go during the night. Once coming down the garden I met the lady going up and she had not quite made it. She said, "Oh dear, I'm a bit late, it's all down my leg and a bootful".'

Mrs Vi Cowley recounts a somewhat unpleasant incident at Lovell Wood Farm in the early 1940s, but no doubt amusing in retrospect. 'Someone left the privy door open one day and a hen fell in the bucket, what a to do! The wife [of the farmer] and I armed ourselves with long sticks and tried levering the bird out, by putting our sticks under her wings, but her legs kept paddling about, and when we eventually rescued her she shook herself and we were plastered. Nothing modern so Maggie and I had to sit in the woodshed while Kitty filled and heated the copper for us to have a "bungalow bath".'

Another lady recalled her wartime wedding day in February 1941. 'My bridegroom was on Embarkation Leave (to the young, that means a week before going abroad with His Majesty's Forces). There had been a sprinkling of snow that made the garden a bit lighter and added to the flashes of search-lights as they passed over High Wycombe three miles away. This helped us as we stumbled down the garden path, never seen before, to the "privy". No lighted window, no street lamps, no torch, so hand in hand we made it! Then back to the cold bed-room and cold water in the jug on the wash-stand. What a romantic evening! Even so we managed 45 years of married life.

'Relating this tale to a friend, she says her husband remembers pushing out the middle of the knot in the wood in the panel and watching his parents both on the double privy on their farm.'

Some people were not shy and did not wait until the privy block was empty before slinking in. Mrs Eileen Hudson of Wraysbury recalls: 'The brighter side was talking to your neigh-bour in the next lav, especially when there were more people using them at the same time and you could pass messages on.'

[8]

PRIVY AND PUBLIC HEALTH: GOVERNMENT GUM-BOOTS STEP IN

As towns grew in size the problems of the disposal of sewage became more and more acute. The rapid expansion and over-crowding of towns and cities in the 19th century produced unbelievable squalor with fetid courts and yards crammed with housing. Often many families shared a single privy whose pit was rarely emptied and a cycle of disease and high mortality rates became the norm. An increasingly concerned government set up commissions and appointed inspectors in the 1840s to inspect these towns and their reports were horrific. In Birmingham for example, privies were 'without doors and overflowing with filth', while their contents were merely dumped in nearby streets.

This sort of thing we are familiar with reading about London or the industrial towns of the Midlands and the North, like Nottingham and Manchester. But there were slums even in Buckinghamshire towns and many survived into the 1930s in Slough, Aylesbury and High Wycombe, for example. High Wycombe is a well documented illustration of what the government was up against in the 1840s in trying to improve the lot of the urban slum dweller. The city fathers saw their primary responsibility as avoiding the need to levy town rates, at whatever cost to their hapless poorer residents.

In the early 19th-century High Wycombe drains and sewage came under the somewhat leisurely eye of the local Paving and Lighting Commissioners, but when Edwin Chadwick's Health of Towns Act was passed in 1848 the town was found to have a mortality rate over the 'acceptable' limit set by the Act of 20 deaths per 1,000. There was bitter opposition to the outside interference of the Board of Health's Inquiry. Newlands, an

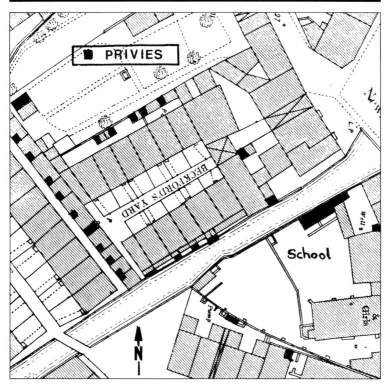

Newlands, High Wycombe in 1875: privies everywhere.

expansion of the town built in low-lying, water-logged mea-
dows, was the main focus where the occupants lived in cramped
courts and alleys among pig sties, dung-heaps and filthy
common privies, but other parts of the town were equally squa-
lid. Witness after intimidated witness reported indescribable
squalor to the Inspector, despite being harried and bullied by
the Council's representatives.

In Bridgewater Yard, for example, 32 people shared the
common privy, not to mention others who used it as a public
convenience. Wells providing drinking water were within yards
of the privy, and occupants contributed to the problem by col-

Newlands in 1934, just before slum clearance. Note the weatherboarded privies overhanging the somewhat unappetising looking river Wye.

lecting dung for re-sale. No wonder the town had frequent outbreaks of typhoid and cholera.

Unfortunately the Inspector's report, condemnatory though it was, could only recommend. Consequently the ratepayers' purses were safeguarded, and improvements only came gradually.

The city fathers finally got round to dealing with the squalor of Newlands when the 1934 Slum Clearance Order was passed. The photographic survey accompanying the Order showed appalling conditions. At Beckford's Yard the tenements backing on to the river had privies overhanging the river Wye while those on the other side of the yard had privies within three feet of their back doors, in yards barely six feet deep. Many privies had been converted to water closets by this time, but the drainage was wholly inadequate and a depressingly large number emptied

Another 1934 photograph taken in Newlands. Privies galore. Note the cricket stumps painted on one privy door: no use retreating there for any peace and quiet!

into cess-pits which seeped out to pollute the watercourses.

In Newlands the slums lasted into the 1930s, but new building gradually improved via a series of Acts of Parliament, notably the 1875 Public Health Act, which laid down minimum standards of, among other things, privy or water closet provision. Indeed, from 1865 local authorities had had to appoint sanitary inspectors and themselves undertake the provision of sewers, drains and refuse disposal: thus emerged the 'lavender cart' so well remembered by many older people.

Rural District Councils and the town councils organised sewage disposal and refuse collection in increasingly efficient ways. Council 'lavender carts' emptied privy pits and cess-pits all over the county and water closets followed in the wake of the provision of mains water. A common practice was for the buckets from bucket privies to be emptied into cess-pools or septic tanks. The council or the landlord then emptied the cess-pit into a tanker lorry and carted the waste away. In Lane End and elsewhere these council workers were, a touch ironically no doubt, known as 'Lavender Jim'.

One of the longest and most interesting reminiscences I received came from an architect, Michael Bayley, who enclosed sketches which are reproduced here. I will not quote his long letter in full but extract the most interesting parts about life in Slough before the Second World War. He was told not to go into New Square, a square of back to back slum dwellings, so naturally as an inquisitive boy he went and looked.

'There was a slum block of cottages where the town's washer-women lived and worked, and a corrugated iron convenience for the men using the adjacent pubs and coach maker's yard. The washerwomen found that the humanly processed beer was an economical substitute for ammonia and used it in their washing – just as had been done in Roman times. Their customers only judged the work on the end product!

'Years later, probably in the 1960s or so, when the cottages had been demolished, the local archaeological society were given permission to dig in the area. They found no trace of lava-tories and drains and couldn't understand how the place had worked – and were not inclined to believe me when I told them!'

Michael Bayley also wrote about middens or rubbish and dung heaps and told me where one survives. 'When you go just beyond Sainsbury's supermarket on the corner of Lake End Road and look towards Dorney, where the road swerves left, you will see someone has planted trees on the long bank of raised ground to the left. The bank is a vast midden of the rub-bish and night soil collected by Slough's dust carts in the 1920s and 30s, which was dumped into the long deep pond in Pond Leys, the remains of a flash lock on one of the medieval canal streams of the Thames from above Taplow Mill.'

Mr Bayley then wrote about the flypaper man, a very neces-

Michael Bayley's drawing of the yard behind a number of pubs in Slough in 1928. The urinal discharged into buckets for the use of the local washer-women.

sary service in days when urban waste heaps were collected infrequently and when privies were cheek by jowl in yards. The smells and the flies were awful, bluebottles of hideous juiciness constantly abuzzing everywhere. 'The district flypaper man did a brisk trade in home-made flypapers – strips of paper smeared with a mixture of black treacle and arsenic, I believe. Most houses were full of bluebottles bred in rubbish bins and middens. I enclose a photocopy of a sketch my father made of him (the flypaper man) as a young man when he (my father) was at a dame school in Slough run by Miss Butt – I can just remember him as an old man when I was small – still using his trademark cry of "Catch 'em alive-oh".'

In the age of the earth closet flies were a constant pest, huge and well fed on privy waste, middens and dung hills! This is a drawing by Michael Bayley's father, made in about 1880, of the district flypaper seller.

At Little Marlow School, built in 1876, the privy blocks were accessed from the school yard beyond the middle distance wall, while the schoolmaster's house had its privy access from the nearer yard.

Few surviving Victorian schools retain their outside privies. In 1868 at Loughton, now within Milton Keynes, the 'outside offices', a standard surveyor's euphemism for privies, cost £32 out of a total building cost of £308. The high cost was due to the need to provide separate facilities for boys and girls. Until recently the privy buildings survived at the 1863 church school at Dagnall, near Ivinghoe. The privy block at Little Marlow school of 1876 survives, but without the innards. It is in a simpler style than the Gothic school building, although the door tops are cut into a central Gothic trefoil. Schoolchildren probably had better toilet facilities at school than at home!

This was probably also the case in the workhouses built after the Poor Law Amendment Act of 1834. Made deliberately unwelcoming to discourage the poor from malingering at the ratepayers' expense, they at least had privies in some numbers for the inmates. The Amersham, Aylesbury, Slough and New-

A pair of privies at Little Marlow School. Note the trefoil cut in the door top: a touch of Gothic to match the more elaborately Gothic school building.

port Pagnell workhouses survive as hospitals, though not their privies, but the Buckingham and Saunderton ones have been almost entirely demolished.

Nowadays all this seems a lifetime away. Public health and private amenities have improved beyond measure and the indoor water closet is universal at all levels of society. I know of no earth closets or bucket privies still in use in Buckinghamshire of necessity.

The buildings I have described and visited and many more that I have, perforce, missed look cosily romantic now but those who used them knew the grimmer reality. As Mrs Vi Cowley of Akeley wrote in her letter to me: 'I can chuckle now, but didn't all those years ago.'

This century has seen enormous changes that have had profound impacts on our lives, such as manned flight, the jet engine, men on the moon and so on as well as spectacular medical advances. However, the universal water closet situated within the house has had just as profound an effect. Nowadays houses may have two or three indoor toilets and still husbands and fathers grumble about being unable to get into them. As I write this I cannot help wondering how my womenfolk would cope with an outside earth closet up the end of the garden and a washstand and jug in the cold bedroom for washing!

Times have changed dramatically and now we look back with nostalgia on earlier times with their privies. We must be grateful though, to public health reformers and their appointed officials and remember the delight with which people occupied the new council houses in town and country with their unheard of luxuries of indoor flushing toilets and baths.

[9]

A SELECTION OF PRIVIES TO SEE IN BUCKINGHAMSHIRE

Privies that you can visit in Buckinghamshire are relatively few and far between but a visit to the Chiltern Open Air Museum, near Chalfont St Peter, is an absolute must. This is a collection of re-erected cottages, farmhouses, barns, granaries and other rescued historic buildings set in the rolling Chiltern hills. It draws its buildings not only from the Chilterns but also from north and south of them and is a fascinating day out for all those interested in their past.

More to the point, it has no less than three privies, beautifully restored, and illustrating much of the best of Buckinghamshire privy building. In fact so well restored are they that occasionally visitors, particularly young ones, assume the privies are the museum's toilet facilities and use them. So I suppose my earlier comment that I know of no privies still in use in the county needs a minor, if unintended, adjustment! There is also a cast-iron public convenience from a Reading tram terminus which is genuinely intended for use by museum visitors.

The list below is not intended to be comprehensive and can, of course, be added to. It is advisable to telephone to check on the opening times which I have summarised as best I can but they vary from year to year. I have only included those that can be seen in houses and museums and not those that can be seen from the road.

There are very many former privies that can be seen from the road. After you have read this book I hope you will become adept at picking them out from some distance and provoking groans from your family: "Not another privy, Dad (or Mum)!"

It should also be noted that the privies mentioned and described in the book are not open to the public. Only those in

Chiltern Open Air Museum: the Wycombe Toll House one-holer.

the list below are, and at the times indicated.

Selected List of Privies/Privy Buildings to Visit

The Amersham Museum, 49 High Street. A medieval hall house. At the end of its long narrow garden, corresponding to its medieval burgage plot, is a double privy backing onto a stream, half serving No 47. Built in brick with a tiled roof its innards do not survive and it is a (locked) store shed. Museum open Saturdays, Sundays and Bank Holidays, Easter to end of October. Wednesday afternoons in August. Telephone: 01494 725754 or 724299.

The Old Gaol Museum, Market Hill, Buckingham. Former gaol with privy in corner of exercise yard, now converted to water closet. Museum open Monday to Saturday (closed Thursdays) and Sunday afternoons in August. Telephone: 01280 823020.

Chiltern Open Air Museum, Newlands Park, Chalfont St Peter. Caversham Public Convenience, a cast-iron public convenience of 1906, made at Saracen Foundry of Walter McFarlane, Glasgow, for the electric tramway terminus at Caversham Bridge, Reading, Berkshire. Re-erected 1987-1991 and in use. **Preston Bissett Privy**, a weatherboarded building with two separate one-holers, complete with authentic old newspaper squares hanging from the wall. **Mercer's Farm, Kingswood**, a two-holer with a child's lower level seat, weatherboard with a slate roof. **High Wycombe Toll House**, a later 19th-century addition to 1826 turnpike cottage. Museum open approximately April to October. Telephone: 01494 872163.

Chenies Manor House, Chenies Village. Tudor Manor House with privies in the Lodgings Range chimney projections of the 1520s. Open April to September, Wednesday and Thursday afternoons, also Bank Holiday Monday afternoons. Telephone: 01494 762888.

Chicheley Hall. c1720 garden building in 'Wilderness' north of canal. Former privy. Innards gone but front bearer beam remains. Open Easter, May and August Bank Holiday Sundays and Mondays and also other Sundays in August, 2.30-5.00. Telephone: 01234 391252.

Pitstone Green Farm Museum, Vicarage Road, Pitstone, near Ivinghoe. Rural and domestic bygones, farm machinery, etc. Has a two-holer seat on display and a urinal. Plans to build privy in near future. Open last Sunday in the month and Bank Holidays, May to September. Telephone: 01296 661997/668223.

Stowe Landscape Gardens. The Shepherds Cote. A privy west of Eleven Acre Lake, 5 metres south of the Queen Caroline Monument. Pyramidal roof and arched frieze. Grounds open daily Easter and Summer school holidays. Term time (April to July, September and October) Monday, Wednesday, Friday and Sunday. Telephone: 01280 822850.

A Privy by Any Other Name

A 'certain' place
Asterroom
Biffy
Bog
Boghouse
Bombay
Chamber of Commerce
Chamberlain pianos ('bucket lav')
Chuggie
Closet
Comfort station
Crapphouse
Crapping castle
Crapping kennel
Dike
Dinkum-dunnies
Dunnekin
Dunnick
Dyke
Doneks
Dubs
Duffs
Garden loo
Garder robe
Gong house
Gong
Go and have a Jimmy Riddle
Go and have a Tim Tit
Going to pick daisies
Going to see a man about a dog
Going to stack the tools
Going to the George
Going to the groves
Going where the wind is always blowing
Heads
Here is are
Holy of holies
Honk
House of commons
House of office
Houses of parliament
Jakes
Jerry-come tumble
Jericho
Karzi
Klondike
Larties
Latrine
Lavatory
Little House
My aunts
Nessy
Netty
Out the back
Petty

Place of easement
Place of repose
Place of retirement
Reading room
Round-the-back
Shit-hole
Shittush
Shooting gallery
Shunkie
Slash house
The backhouse
The boggy at the Bottom
The bush
The dispensary
The dunny
The grot
The halting station Hoojy-boo
  (attributed to Dame Edith
  Evans)
The house where the emperor
  goes on foot
The hum
The jakes
The jampot
The japping
The John
The lats
The long drop
The opportunity
The ping-pong house
The proverbial
The Sammy
The shants
The shot-tower
The sociable

The tandem (a two holer)
The thinking house
The throne room
The watteries
The wee house
The whajucallit
Three and more seaters
Thunder box
Two seaters
Widdlehouse
Windsor Castle
'Yer Tiz'

Especially for WCs:
Adam & Eve
Chain of events
Flushes and blushes
The penny house
The plumbing
The porcelain pony
The water box
Umtag (Russian version of the
  WC)
Going to inspect the plumbing
The urinal
Waterloo

The term 'privy' is an Early
  Middle English word which
  derives from the Latin
  'privatus' meaning apart or
  secret.

ACKNOWLEDGEMENTS

Thank you to everyone who so willingly allowed me to photograph their privies, to those who told me tales, to those who responded to the pieces in the local papers, and to the local newspaper editors for their articles.

To many of you who may remember Sir Bernard Miles' short film on Chiltern Privies made in the 1950s, which first put the (south) Buckinghamshire privy on the map, this book is a successor.

Thank you to Nicholas Battle, my publisher, for his help and encouragement and above all thank you to my wife Jill, and family to whom this book is lovingly dedicated.

Acknowledgements are also due to the Wycombe Local History and Chair Museum for permission to use the photographs from Wycombe's 1934 Slum Clearance report; Roger Evans for the photograph of the Coleshill privy at Littlelands, and Julia Smith for the photograph of Mad Arthur's indoor privy at Winslow; Michael Bayley for his drawings of the flypaper man and the Slough pub urinals.